In the Boat

Written by Paul Shipton
Illustrated by Trevor Dunton

Collins

1

One mouse in the boat.

Taxi

Two rabbits in the boat.

Taxi

Three cats in the boat.

Taxi

4

Four dogs in the boat.

Taxi
Taxi

Five elephants in the boat.

Six fish in the boat!

In the Boat

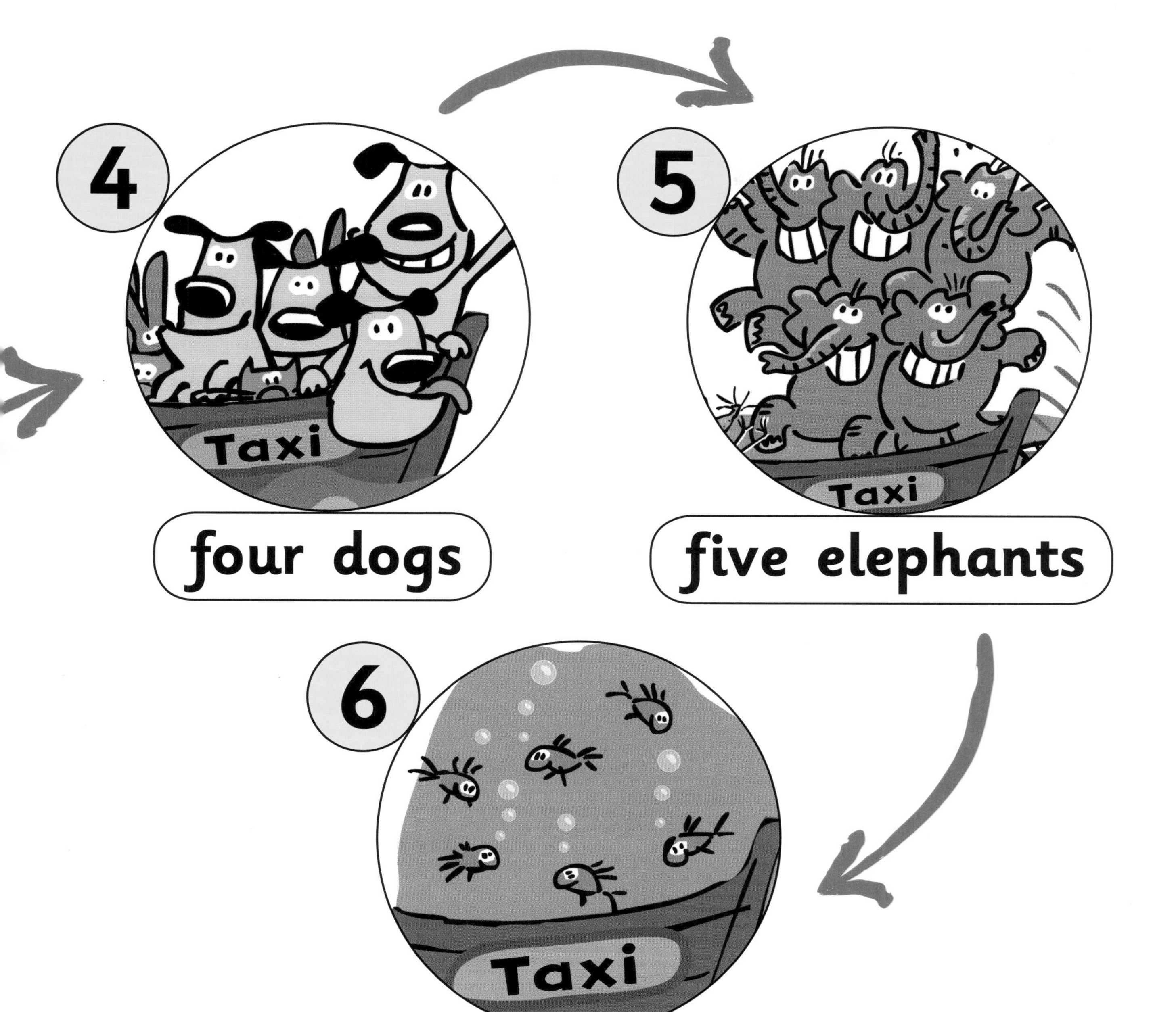

six fish

Ideas for reading

Written by Clare Dowdall, PhD
Lecturer and Primary Literacy Consultant

Reading objectives:
- read some common irregular words
- use phonic knowledge to decode regular words and read them aloud accurately
- read and understand simple sentences
- demonstrate understanding when talking with others about what they have read

Communication and language objectives:
- follow instructions involving several ideas or actions
- listen to stories, accurately anticipating key events and respond to what they hear with relevant comments
- develop their own narratives and explanations by connecting ideas or events

Curriculum links: Mathematical Development; Knowledge and Understanding of the World

High frequency words: one, two, three, four, five, six, in, is, the, who

Interest words: one, two, three four, five, mouse, rabbits, cats, dogs, elephants, fish, taxi

Resources: cards with number words from one to six, a large dice

Word count: 30

Build a context for reading

- Roll the dice and ask the children to shout out the number. Roll again and ask them to find the matching number word.
- Practise reading all the number words, focusing on the initial sounds and word shape.
- Look at the front cover together and discuss what this story might be about. Read the word *taxi* and ask the children if they have ever been in one.
- Read the title together. Model tracing the words from left to right with your finger, and sounding out and blending the phonemes in *boat*.
- Ask the children to predict what might happen in this story.

Understand and apply reading strategies

- Read pp1–3 together. Read the word *one*. Look for the number 1 on the page. Ask the children for examples of one thing that is in the picture, e.g. *one fish, one taxi, one sign*.